I wish I ~~had been your~~ born from you

Poems and reflections on adoption

KAREN LOMAS

Published by
British Association for Adoption & Fostering
(BAAF)
Saffron House
6–10 Kirby Street
London EC1N 8TS
www.baaf.org.uk

Charity registration 275689 (England and Wales)
and SC039337 (Scotland)

British Library Cataloguing in Publication Data
A catalogue record for this book is available
from the British Library

ISBN 978 1 905664 83 2

Designed and typeset by Helen Joubert Design
Printed in Great Britain by The Lavenham Press
Trade distribution by Turnaround Publisher Services,
Unit 3, Olympia Trading Estate, Coburg Road,
London N22 6TZ

BAAF is the leading UK-wide membership organisation
for all those concerned with adoption, fostering and
child care issues.

Contents

■

This book is dedicated to the memory
of my beautiful mother who taught me how to love
and sadly never met my daughter Emily.

It is for all those who have lovingly and courageously
chosen to have a family by adoption.
It is also for their families and friends, as well as for our own.

■

My thanks

My thanks go to Emily's devoted father by adoption for the continued support and love he offers; to friends and family; to those who cared for Emily before she came to us and, in particular, her foster carer and her family. Heartfelt thanks also go to Shaila Shah at BAAF for her belief in my vision and for her support in publishing this book; to Hedi Argent for helping to edit and shape the book; to all at the Post Adoption Centre; and to Helen Kahn and Nicky Jones for their brilliant support.

Most of all my thanks go to Emily, my amazing daughter whose "mama" I am genuinely privileged to be. Thank you Emily, for all the love and happiness you have given me. To use your words to me,

'I love you the whole world and all the planets and all the stars.'

Foreword

I Wish I Had Been Born From You, a collection of poems and reflections by Karen Lomas, captures one woman's journey to adopt and to help her daughter adjust and attach after she joins their family by adoption.

Karen's words express in eloquent prose and poems poignant challenges and triumphs of the adoptive journey. While each person's journey is unique, many themes and experiences of adoption are universal. Karen explores universal themes in a way that touches the reader. This collection is a unique and powerful affirmation for those already on this path.

I Wish I Had Been Born From You is a remarkable resource for professionals preparing prospective parents for building their families through adoption. Karen speaks to all of us touched by adoption. I well remember when my daughter, who joined my family by adoption, expressed the same sentiment: 'Mommy,' she said, 'I wish I had been born to you'. I have spent years working to teach parents and professionals the ins and outs of this journey. Karen Lomas teaches all of us by touching our hearts and souls with her words.

Holly van Gulden
October 2009

■

Opening the door

Fabulous and feral
Feisty and feline
Given to fury
Against a wall

People misunderstanding
Projects perplexing
Routines unfamiliar
Foundations not laid

Our job: To spot them
Remove them
Build a doorway
Keep it clear

■

1

Opening the door

Opening the door was written this year, almost seven years since we adopted our lovely daughter Emily.

The "wall" in the poem is the defensive one she sometimes builds for herself when she faces challenges that appear too difficult for her. Her frustrations are further exacerbated by the fact that she has physically reached puberty, whilst emotionally, she still continues to regress at times.

It has been, and continues to be, our job to help provide her with the strategies she needs and thus to attempt to minimise her frustrations; to "open the doors" by trying to provide the tools to enable her to cope better. We are privileged to do so.

2

The quilt

My daughter posed for the camera in her Grandma's very green garden, the pink, floral patchwork filling her arms.

'I've made quilts for all my grandchildren. It's taken me three months to make Emily's off and on. I wanted to treat her the same as the others.'

I was so moved by her generosity and the way she had so quickly taken our daughter to her heart. We met Granny Sue, mother of four by adoption, on a holiday at the time when we were being approved as adopters and we instantly became friends. She was delighted to agree to become our daughter's "honorary" grandma.

On the train home Emily said she'd like to make her own patchwork bedcover for Lily, her favourite cuddly toy.

Every night for months after receiving the quilt, Emily beamed with the love that she knew had been sewn into every patch and would bring the quilt to her face as if hugging a loved one and say, 'My Granny Sue made this specially for me.'

Poetry reading and writing with my daughter, as well as alone, has been like creating a patchwork-quilt. A quilt that can reflect personality, interests and experiences and is always a labour of love involving choices and discoveries. Quilts are made to last, often passed down through the generations and alive with the memories of the maker and the receiver. And, just like the patches in a quilt, working out which patches complement each other is like working out how to insert the "patch" my daughter might need next.

—■—

3

Where the poetry came from

Seven years ago my partner and I met Emily, a disturbed, sickly and frightened little seven-year-old. One of four siblings, her two younger sisters had been placed for adoption together, but following assessment it was decided to place Emily and her elder brother separately due to the severity and long duration of their neglect and, in Emily's case, the serious health problems that resulted.

We had initially wanted a younger child, knowing how hard it would be to establish a solid relationship in a few short years before the onset of puberty. The educational psychologist spoke to us of attachment disorder and early promiscuity, whilst stressing that if Emily could feel valued as a member of our family, and form a genuine attachment to us, these problems might not arise in the future, or be less serious. One thing was clear, however, to all the agencies and people that assessed Emily, and especially to her very experienced foster carer, with whom she lived for three-and-a-half years: Emily's behaviour would always be extremely challenging.

There was only one question she asked us: 'Are you,' she said, quite sharply, 'prepared to be embarrassed?'

We were so taken aback by what might have been construed as an unkind remark that we did not ask her to elucidate but replied, somewhat over-confidently, 'We don't get embarrassed; people can think what they like. Where we live, people don't bother anyway – it's a big town.'

It was a few months later before we realised exactly what she had meant. Our daughter is extremely affectionate but her fight to survive, quite literally, and her frailty due to abuse, including starvation, had almost killed her before she was taken into care. When it was discovered that she needed major heart surgery, her chances of surviving the operation were very much in doubt. Her two brushes with death have further fuelled her indomitable spirit, which makes her extraordinarily strong-willed and stubborn. Add to this her impulsiveness and need to dominate, and you have a real force with which to reckon, particularly when this translates into show-stopping tantrums in the middle of the supermarket or in the street!

Establishing a family by adoption might be viewed as an "artificial" exercise. In our case, my partner and I had been each other's family for almost two decades and had weathered the various storms of life together including parent death, career changes and childlessness, and we knew how to support and help one another. Welcoming Emily into our lives and creating a solid family unit with the three of us was a challenge we embraced positively, whilst acknowledging that there would be some difficult times ahead. Not only was Emily one of four siblings, but she had also been in foster care with other children and we quickly became sensitive to the fact that she found it uncomfortable at times to be the only child in the family, as well as the "newcomer".

Emily's desire to build a father-daughter bond and a mother-daughter bond developed quite naturally. This enabled us to share our particular interests with her and for her to enjoy the sole attention of either her mum or dad, one at a time. Emily's dad is artistic whereas I barely recognise one end of a paintbrush from the other. In our "exclusive" mother-daughter time, we went swimming (Emily's favourite thing!), cooked, baked and began to share the reading and writing of poetry.

It's perhaps important to say at this point that poetry wasn't a tool I had up my sleeve when we thought about parenting our daughter. It has really been a case of stumbling across this very useful outlet. On the advice of a work colleague who had adopted a daughter, I began keeping a diary. I soon got frustrated, however, because even though I kept in mind that it should be brief, I was still quite daunted by the task and felt that it was actually adding to the stress of dealing with our exceptionally challenging daughter. Every time I made an entry and noted that the previous one had been several weeks or months before, I felt I had failed somehow, particularly as I definitely wanted some written record of this incredibly unique event in my life.

One day, before her eighth birthday, when she had been with us for about six months, Emily brought home a poem, which she had painted in class. It was on a large sheet of paper and it looked so bright and cheerful and the words, too, showed Emily's positive feelings about joining our family. The teacher had simply told her to think about what adoption meant to her by creating a line for each letter of the word "ADOPTION". The poem was one of the first real insights into Emily's feelings, and the last line, especially, moved me to tears. Emily was extremely proud of it – we pinned it up on the kitchen door and then, two years later, when we had a party to celebrate the legal adoption, we displayed it and read it out loud. Her pride and sense of achievement were obvious and she said she wanted to write more.

This was even more encouraging since Emily has a Statement of Special Learning Needs and has problems with reading and writing, although she is always full of brilliant ideas. To help her, reading poems seemed to offer "bite-size" chunks, which she enjoyed; then we began to start making up our own, just out loud, enjoying the sounds, making up a line each, creating nonsense verse mostly, but having fun together. Sometimes we'd set each other a challenge like "Summer", "Football", "Happiness", "What Makes Me Angry", or we'd take a poem we'd read, say about a dad, then we'd spend time thinking about her dad and rewrite it to make it personal to our family. We'd write a verse for each other and then read them aloud. It was like giving each other "hand-made" gifts, especially as Emily sometimes decorated hers with pictures. Like the paintings done with her dad, we'd later enjoy sharing these as a family.

Once we had begun writing poems together, I liked to spend time reflecting and making sense of something that had happened during the day by also writing it into a poem.

The poems in this book reveal the joys and the pain of our journey to become a family through adoption. Since our shared poems were simply for fun, and most didn't get written down, they are mainly my poems rather than my daughter's, although I have also included some heartfelt notes and cards written by Emily.

Her poem, *Adoption,* was the catalyst for what followed and was thus the original inspiration for this book.

———■———

Adoption

by Emily, age 7

A family gets together

Days are good

Only just got to know them

Put some candles on a cake

Think I'm going to like it here

I can be happy

Only 1 day to go

Nobody knows how good it feels

4

Thinking of adopting...

'I used to be frightened of the Tube when I was a little boy because of the Yetis in Doctor Who.' It is late in the evening. My friend, David, adds, 'Do you remember them too?' I nod and smile. His train arrives and then, quite out of the blue, he says, 'Jane and I are thinking of adopting; we can't have children either.' He goes; the doors close. His train moves towards the tunnel and I wave.

I am left to ponder the difficulties couples have in making the decision to adopt, in coming to terms with their own inability to conceive or their choice not to conceive their own children, or to increase their existing family through adoption. It is then that I decide I would like to share my poems and reflections and this book is born.

My mind also flashes back to one of the first exchanges I had with an experienced adoptive parent: 'We're thinking of adopting. Any advice?' 'Run for the hills!' my colleague joked, but added, 'It's been difficult, still is, and Cheryl still doesn't really have a relationship with her dad. That's been hard, particularly for him, but it's still the best thing I've ever done.'

That afternoon, somewhat nervously, I made the first call to our local fostering and adoption service and registered our interest.

■

Under the microscope

First, do you meet our criteria?
Are you white?
Black, brown, gay or straight, or other?
Married, single
In a relationship of any kind?

Employed or unemployed?
Able-bodied or disabled?
Young, middle-aged or old?
Are you in good health?
Are your parents still alive?

Do you have birth children?
How long did you try?
Any miscarriages?
Infertility? IVF?
So, why do you want to adopt?

Do you have a good support network?
People to call upon when you need them?
Is your relationship solid?
Can it be pushed to the limits
By the demands this child will place upon it?

Will you accept
A child who has been abused,
Is disabled?
Mentally, physically, has ADHD
Is partially sighted or deaf?

Would you consider one child or more?
A boy or a girl –
Why's that?
We're not insinuating
(Just need to be sure...

You're not some kind of dysfunctional pervert.)
Could you deal with faeces smeared
On the wall of your home?
With damage and tantrums?
With birth parent contact?

Are you prepared
For the drugs and the drink and
Sexual promiscuity?
For anger and violence
Or rejection?

You see we have to be sure
That there isn't,
Well, any more
That you haven't said.
We need to probe in deep.

We need to be sure you are strong,
Have the stamina, the energy
The patience, the money, the time, the space, the safe home
The family, the friends
You will need.

It isn't easy, of course not, but if we approve you,
After months of probing and preparation
In session after session,
You will be matched,
And then, you will, in time,
Take her home.

■

5

Becoming an approved adopter

'We'd like a baby,' said the smiling couple sat opposite us in the circle.

'I want two toddlers, twins if possible.' This time the voice was that of a young woman who was choosing to parent as a single mum. The "baby" couple mentioned IVF and being rather apprehensive. The "twins" woman said she was an educational psychologist and had absolutely no doubts whatsoever about having a family by adoption. We said we wanted a slightly older child – preferably a girl, over three, and that we did feel we had a lot more to learn and felt quite nervous about having a family this way. We all confided that we felt "on show"; like we had to be on our best behaviour, for example, opting for the fruit rather than the biscuits to show we knew about being healthy!

'At the moment there are 50,000 children in the UK awaiting adoption,' we were told, still believing, albeit momentarily, that we might end up in competition for a particular child; like the "one-off" sale at Selfridges, for which people camp out! I chastised myself for the comparison but when the "catalogue" of children, enticingly entitled *Be My Parent*, was shown around by the social worker, it didn't help to dispel the idea that these children were being "marketed".

Under the microscope was partly about emotionally releasing myself from a process which I had mostly found thought-provoking and interesting but also highly intrusive. At times, it angered me and I make no apologies for reflecting this in the bitter sarcasm of the poem.

I've heard some potential adopters describe the process of being assessed as being 'psychoanalysed'! It certainly gets you thinking – firstly about why the thousands of parents whose children have been taken into care don't have to get approved before they have another baby; then, more calmly, about all the things that you need to have in place and to deal with in order to function effectively as "good enough" parents (as opposed to aspiring to be super mum and dad!). I hope it will bring a smile of recognition if you have already begun, or been through this process. It's important to note here that our adoption social worker was sensitive, diplomatic and understanding and she endeavoured to make the process as comfortable as possible. *Under the microscope*, which she has already read, is by no means intended as a criticism of her skills.

———■———

Our Welsh princess

She came from the valleys in purple plastic mules
and princess costumes,
Her blue eyes looked haunted,
Her Labrador leap down the stairs and into our arms,
The over-joyous shouts of 'Mammy!' 'Daddy!'
As she embraced us; two complete strangers,
Set the alarm bells ringing in our heads.

She was tall and reed thin.
She was wild and in pain.

Could we make her feel better again?

We took her out; this strange, feral creature,
Light as a toddler, and too desperate to please.
In the park her painted face was a pale-pink butterfly.
We bought her ice-cream, jumped together over the waves,

Wrote her name in the sand; and as she erased it
The alarm bells rang loudly in our heads.

She was tall and reed thin.
She was wild and in pain.

Could we ever make her feel better again?

We brought her home for the first time.
And, swinging happily on the tatty seat,
Curled in the sun under a paling canopy,
We watched our princess' fake finery slip away;
The girl beneath revealed; smiling,
Ringing the bells in our hearts.

■

6

Introductions: Meeting our daughter for the first time

For the next two years we trawled the "catalogue" and time after time had our hopes dashed because a child had already "gone". Unlike the plasma TV screen you didn't get at the lowest price in the sale, these disappointments did hurt – a great deal at times – and getting over them was by no means easy.

In fact, in the end, we didn't choose but were actually chosen to be our daughter's parents: the National Adoption Register database had just come into being and we were selected by her local authority. Our social worker phoned us and we found her picture in the "catalogue" and were uncertain. It was not, as I have heard a number of other adoptive parents say, "love at first sight". It was much more a case of 'If we don't try, this might never happen and she just *might* be our perfect daughter. We can't make a decision based on one tiny photo of a sweet smiling girl bearing a toothless grin and one very brief paragraph. We need to find out more...'

On the day we were to meet our daughter and she was to meet her "forever" mummy and daddy for the very first time, we left early and drove excitedly to the foster carer's house. This was to be an hour's visit to the home only.

We passed in front of the large clean window and noticed the cat on top of the armchair. It was Monday, 2pm, the last week in May, and my heart was pounding as we knocked on the front door. It opened and a tall, grey-haired smiling woman with spectacles invited us in, her broad Welsh accent already familiar to us from the meeting with her some weeks before.

As soon as we came through the door, Emily leapt down the stairs with her arms open wide yelling 'Mammy! Daddy!' Emily's "charm offensive" and her desperate need to please were the second things that struck us once we had overcome the completely unexpected greeting. It was more what you would expect from the child of wealthy jet-setters who had been left with a governess whilst they were away on an extended holiday; it certainly had a touch of the Disney about it with Emily dressed in her princess costume and high-heeled mules! In fact, we later realised that Emily's ideas of family were very much the stuff of the many idealised cartoons she saw in her Disney DVDs.

She had been prepared for adoption by her foster carer and by the book we had put together to introduce ourselves, our home and our lives. A social worker was, at this very late stage, helping Emily to produce her own life story book in readiness for her move to her "forever Mammy and Daddy".

She hugged each of us in turn in the most flamboyant manner you can imagine, teetering on her sparkling heels as she reached up to us both.

The foster carer showed us into the front room, removing the cat as she did so. We soon got down onto the floor to talk to this bubbly, chatty little girl. The social worker had advised us to bring a present and I had chosen a book of fairy jigsaws. We completed these together and then, after turning down Emily's suggestion of watching a video, telling her we'd prefer to play, chatted about her favourite things and our plans for the next day. The hour flew. Tomorrow we would have two hours and we told Emily that we would be picking her up and taking her to the park; she seemed delighted. Then we watched her eyes glaze over again as she clicked the remote to put on a DVD before we had even left the room.

Afterwards, buzzing with a mass of thoughts and feelings we went back to the hotel, our home for the week. Our social worker rang that evening, and we talked through our initial impressions. She was, as ever, the voice of calm, saying that she was certain we would do a brilliant job of parenting this lovely little girl. However, we remained uncertain and more than a little scared in the face of the biggest decision of our whole lives! Given Emily's Disney world vision of family life, would we be the right King and Queen for the Princess? Was the Princess the right one for us?

The rest of the week we got to know each other over several portions of Emily's favourite blackcurrant cheesecake, frequent trips to our hotel's jacuzzi and pool with our mermaid, rolling down a grassy mound at the front of the hotel (well, Emily and her dad at any rate!), a day on the beach, playing in the sea, trips to the local park.

We also visited her teacher, the educational psychologist, the school nurse and had long chats with her foster carer to find out more. At the end of the first introductions week, we learned that our daughter had a diagnosis of ADHD (attention deficit hyperactivity disorder), although the social worker thought it might "simply" be environmental and "disappear" once Emily was in a settled environment. There had been no mention of this in her file. At least it went some way to explaining her 30-second concentration span!

———■———

Snowdrop

Fragile and delicate
like a snowdrop,
a line of thread.
A breeze might take you
and your pretty skirt of hair.
Robust and adaptable —
like sand into pearl,
trapped beneath the collapsing canopy.
You have proved it,
over and over again:
You have been
Hidden
Trodden
Revived
Uprooted
Divided
Separated
Placed
There.
There!
There?
Here.
There, there,
where the fairies cushion your dreams.

7

Getting to know one another

■

By the end of the first week of introductions, we knew that "our princess" was the perfect one for us and she had won our hearts.

We brought her home for the first time, the weekend prior to her permanent move to join our family. She was excited to recognise the green front door from our book. We showed her around the house and into her new bedroom. She immediately fell prostrate and kissed the duvet cover and the matching picture of fairies specially painted by my niece onto glass, and hanging on the wall opposite her bed. We folded Granny Sue's quilt to fit across the bottom of her bed so that she could still see her yellow duvet with its "glow in the dark" pink and lilac fairies.

She placed our life story book in her bedside cabinet. We then looked at her own life story book, finished in a hurry during our introductions fortnight. On the fourth page Emily had written: 'They stole me from my Mammy and Daddy'. Her words choked me. I held her close and hid my tears behind her back. When I eventually looked into her eyes, deciding that it was, in fact, honest to show her how much I cared, she looked back at me tenderly and said, 'Don't cry, Mammy; it's OK now'.

I realised then, even more fully, what I had known from the outset – our pencil-thin princess was loyal and compassionate and a remarkable survivor.

Details of our daughter's struggle to survive troubled me greatly. During the first three-and-a-half years of her life, she almost died. Twice. Once due to starvation and neglect and once owing to major heart surgery.

Later that day we were walking through our market. 'Will you buy me some baby cabbages?' she asked, pointing at the enormous pile of sprouts on the stall. Trying not to show my surprise in case it might change her mind, I replied, 'Sprouts? Yes, of course. What would you like with them?'

'I'd just like you to cook them for me.'

'What? A few, you mean?

'No, a plateful on their own – I love sprouts!' Her face beamed. We returned home and she did indeed devour the whole plateful with relish!

In fact, the weekend went so well that the planned introductions programme was altered and Emily stayed. We did take her back the following Thursday for the farewell party with her foster carer and family and, exceptionally, the three of us were allowed a family room in the hotel. The following day we brought our daughter home to join us permanently.

After hearing one day on the radio that a snowdrop, although it looks dainty, fragile and pure, is exceptionally robust and can cope with being roughly handled, moved about and still thrive, I wrote *Snowdrop*. The characteristic resemblance to our very tall and slender daughter with her then blond bob, who had survived terrible neglect and frequent upheaval, seemed a perfect metaphor.

Happy Birthday

Have a lovly
day

TO the best mum in the world

Happy Birthday

Here is a kiss for you

Roses are red
vilet are blue
Sugar is sweet
and your definitely
sweet to me

Lots of love

x x x

■

Gift

One day, quite out of the blue,
You said,
'I wish I had been born from you,'
I replied,
'Me too'.

■

Treasure

The word comes out of my mouth
when I address you without
any idea that it will
and simply because you are ...
My Treasure

■

8

The "honeymoon": Bringing our child home forever

Parents everywhere call their children by warm endearments – darling, sweetheart, and so forth. We talk about the "gift" of a new life; the miracle. Being given the opportunity to have a child through adoption inspires all those very powerful feelings of overwhelming love, amazement, joy and gratitude.

The poem *Gift* was born out of two conversations with my daughter. Our introductions week included my birthday. Emily asked her foster carer for a present to give me; her foster carer told her that *she* was my gift and I needed no other. When my daughter then repeated this to me, I added, 'the best and most precious gift ever'.

One day, when we were both elbow-deep in pastry and truly relaxed in each other's company, we shared a beautiful and perfect moment. The exact words of our conversation became the short poem, *Gift*.

Emily's social worker described the journey we would make with our daughter, telling us that there would be a "honeymoon" period when everything would be wonderful and our child would be on her best behaviour. She was right: there were idyllic moments in the garden, in the park, at home with a smiling, loving child who could not help enough in the kitchen, who wanted to dust and clean floors, who kissed every single thing in her room, every surface, every packet in the supermarket with the sheer joy of having her own home, her own things and her own family. The kissing of everything went on for some time as did her genuine appreciation of every gift, every new item of clothing. It was endearing, and at the same time slightly disturbing, as it was so extreme and, just occasionally, there were signs that it was a "performance"; that she was trying so hard, too hard, to be everything she thought she should be so that she would "keep us".

Emily longed for the legal adoption and the strain of the wait was apparent. She would talk about it a lot and it was clear, despite endless reassurances, that she was expecting rejection every time she did something "wrong". Her impulsivity meant that she did make mistakes, as everyone does, and we always tried to make light of genuine accidents, but her fear and low self-esteem, as well as her expectation of rejection, were stronger.

After upsets when we'd have to discipline her, she would push notes under the dining-room door to say she was sorry or that she loved us, or they would just say, 'I want my Mama and Dada'. She would scream the same words in the most disturbing and heart-rending of tearful outbursts.

Then there was the 'I want to go home' phrase, used frequently when she was distressed at being sent to her bedroom, and she explained "home" as wherever we were in the house. In fact, although she helped to decorate her room and loved everything in it, she hardly ever spent time in there alone. It took four years for her to really "own" it as well as to feel that we wouldn't forget her if she wasn't constantly in our presence.

> Dear mama,
>
> I am very sorry for what I did this morning. I do love you a lot. you are the best mum. in the world. baba was very bad a but i will be good :) tonight. love you.

The second short poem here, *Treasure,* is also about these special endearments we use for our children. There was nothing affected about the way I started to call my daughter "treasure" – it just came out quite involuntarily one day and stuck because that is precisely what she feels like to me – the most important thing in my life: my treasure.

One night, after making up a story with her various cuddly toys and using different voices for each of them, I covered her favourite leopard with the mini patchwork duvet we had sewn together and, with the voice I had given her, I said, 'Goodnight, Mama,' and my daughter replied, 'Night, night, Lily'.

I then said, 'Goodnight, my precious,' and she replied with a beautiful beaming smile, 'I thought I was your treasure; I like it when you say that.' 'Goodnight, my treasure. Sweet dreams.'

She gave me the happiest look ever; a look that showed how special and important the word had made her feel.

'I love you, mama.' She had said it before but this time I knew she truly felt it. 'I love you too, Emily.' I kissed her goodnight once more and as I left her room I felt a surge of deep contentment at the absolute joy of being her mum. Things could not have felt more perfect.

—■—

■

My own

Do you gloat and feel smug
Because yours is blood of your blood
Flesh of your flesh
And mine was born to someone else?

Do you accept her truly as an innocent?
Or like some underling thing?
Never once do you say she is lovely
My beautiful precious girl.

Not blood of my blood
Nor flesh of my flesh
And yet, my own

■

9

Reactions from family and friends

The advice from the social workers was to introduce our daughter to family and friends gradually and only after a three-month period so that she would not be faced with too many demands at once. Emily loved meeting her new family and making new friends but her behaviour did alter significantly – and not always for the better.

On one occasion when visiting, Emily disappeared to the toilet and was gone some time. We had just got home after the visit when the phone rang to tell me that some chocolates had been taken. Emily was distressed at being found out and it took some time before she would admit it. Whilst to us this was recognised and expected behaviour, indeed almost par for the course, to our friend it was perceived as our failure to "control" our daughter and a sign that she was deliberately naughty.

Sometimes, seeing strangers respond to our daughter without understanding the background responsible for her actions was hurtful but understandable. Hearing her harshly chastised by, and listening to comments from those who knew more and should have known better, cut us to the core.

In some cases, family members not making the effort to visit and welcome our new daughter, as I had consistently welcomed their new arrivals into the family, regardless of distance or other commitments, also hurt us.

One night, feeling let down, I sat down and poured out my bitterness into two poems, *My Own* and *Survival*. The second is loosely modelled on the Shakespearean sonnet which inspired it: 'Shall I compare thee to a summer's day?' with 12 rather than 14 lines, as the form suited the mood I was in at the time and my desire to distance myself from the injustice I believed Emily was suffering.

In the cold light of day, rationality returned and I took stock and realised that communication is key: I had to tell my friends and family more about her needs; I couldn't expect them to understand her in the way that we did. I also wanted to know how they felt and the book meant that I had an excuse to invite them to write down their thoughts honestly.

A few of these follow.

Reactions from family and friends – in their own words

'My true feelings about having an adopted cousin were mixed in the beginning. I remember being concerned before Emily arrived about how easily she would fit into the family and how things would change. Knowing she had her own problems, would she cope with a new life and would they be able to find ways around this and also, purely selfishly, I wondered how our relationship would change...

Survival

Do you compare her to your birth child?
You feel perhaps she will not do.
She is more hurt, stubborn and wild,
Than any daughter born to you.
Sometimes from afar your scathing eye does look
And often is her goodness overshadowed
Her qualities ignored by your parent book
Which boasts your child's every virtue out loud.
But she will thrive, my lively loving girl
And when from that skin for which I grieve
Her slumbering snake does steadily unfurl
Her potent strengths you will perceive.

'I was expecting it to be difficult in the beginning to form a bond with Emily as I was warned about certain aspects of her behaviour. Yet I do not remember feeling awkward or difficult; after just a few months Emily was so loveable and a welcome addition to the family...

'Emily is very aware of her adoption and there are no secrets and I think that the way in which it is celebrated and talked about makes it more special and something that we can all appreciate. Adoption is something to be celebrated and should be treated as a second chance for parents and child alike to have the family they deserve.'

☐

'Astrid, my daughter, was then just two-and-a-half months old. Emily formed an immediate bond with Astrid, lifting her deftly from her pram on first meeting and walking off with her with an air of ownership! She was very capable and involved herself in all aspects of Astrid's care; changing nappies, dressing her, playing and chattering with her in wonderful "baby talk". She even chastised her lovingly when Astrid grabbed at her hair. It was a magical thing to watch and surprising to see a young girl taking the care of this tiny baby entirely in her stride. Astrid was so content with her "Auntie" and loved this new source of affection.

'Knowing of Emily's background from Karen, it was all the more moving to see her gentle care of Astrid and their obvious connection. Throughout the visit Emily made reference to her own lack of nurturing as a baby. This really impacted on us. She even told my husband how lucky Astrid was to have such loving parents and to be so well looked after, things we had naively taken for granted as the right of every child.'

☐

'I suppose we all had to make adjustments and no doubt there were feelings of loss and jealousy, particularly for my daughter who is Karen's god-daughter. We had to learn and adjust to the new focus in our friends' lives. We also needed to get to know Emily...

TO,

Mam and DAD
I dont want
to Leve
you

'Five years on from that day, I believe Emily has brought us closer
together. We are both families now and can both appreciate the trials
and tribulations of family life as well as its joy. We have been on several
holidays together and have shared some very enjoyable times. We have
grown to love Emily. She is as much a part of our friends' lives as our
daughter is of ours.'

———■———

My eleven-year-old three-year-old

She fails to get her own way
Offers cuddles
To avoid the discipline that must guide her,
Help her,
But which is always a battle to impose.

The face contorts, the tears flood
The eleven-year-old is supplanted
By the three-year-old
Who lives inside her some of the time
And now outside her less of the time.

And she screams at me:
'I don't love you any more; You're not my mummy!'
She storms, literally, out of the room.
Futile a request not to slam the door!
We have seen this so many times before.

'I don't want you — go away!' she screams.
I look at her, eye to eye, and tell her, calmly, 'I won't'.
Then, her primal, plaintive cry,
'Mammy, Mammy, I want to go home.'
She comes to me and I hug her.
I tell her that she is home, that I love her.
Her tears stop, the shouting ceases,
Her long body moulds itself foetus-like into my lap.
She says, 'I *do* love you, Mama.'
And my heart breaks once more.

■

10

Regression and bonding

'Will you buy me a baby bottle?'

I looked at my almost eight-year-old daughter standing amidst the tightly packed clothes rails. 'You don't really want a baby bottle, do you? Aren't you too old?'

'I want one, I want to drink my milk from it at night.'

Since joining our family, Emily had drunk enough milk to qualify for having her own cow tethered in our tiny back garden! I could barely keep up with buying it.

I hesitated, unsure if I was doing the right thing – whether I should be discouraging her and encouraging her to grow up. But then I looked at her, remembered her history and the social worker saying that she may need to regress, and I decided that this was something she needed to work through. At the till she produced a pack of two Winnie the Pooh dummies. 'I like dummies, can I have these as well?'

Before I could say that I thought dummies might damage her front teeth, and thinking how much I disliked dummies, she looked at me pleadingly, 'They help me to sleep.'

After I had paid for them, and not bought the clothes I thought we were going to choose, she snuggled up to my waist, moving her head up and down on my side like a contented cat.

She wanted to use the bottle for every milk drink and for a while we let her, realising she had never been weaned. Sometimes she would ask me to feed her and she would use baby talk while she took the bottle. Sometimes this was "put on" and sometimes my seven, then eight, then nine-year-old would genuinely regress in front of my eyes: the tall skinny girl would adopt a foetal position in my lap and start communicating in every sense exactly like a baby. In fact, the bottle didn't go completely until she was 11, and the dummies still make an occasional reappearance as does the baby talk.

At a training session I attended, a highly experienced child psychotherapist and an adoptive parent herself, Holly Van Gulden, advised not to hurry the "growing back up". She said, 'Adopted children will grow back up, but in their own time; there's no such thing as too slowly, but too quickly can be harmful'.

Emily loves water. Bath time in her first years with us was a real occasion: lots of bubbles, a classical CD playing from the adjacent room, dolls galore, a bright yellow snorkel and mask, shells and other toys! Me, sitting on the side ready to wash her hair and being invited to buy a drink, usually a "frascati" at her "Mermaid Café", then pretending to drink the cup of foaming bath water before tipping it discreetly down the sink and exclaiming, 'Delicious. I'd like another, please'. When Emily was a bit less polite, I'd mention the smiling mermaid and she'd say, 'Oh, that's my sister next door!'

■

Bath time

by Emily

Cinderella music
For my café
Underwater.
Toys and bubbles in
My home swimming pool.
Me the kind mermaid
Not the bad sister.
Serving my Mama.

■

■

Adoption party

A painted banner in the centre of the hall
A history of three years together on the wall.

Balloons and pink heart cushions scattered
Smiling friends and family who mattered.

A pile of gifts and cards on the table
'Save them 'til later, if you're able!'

A huge adoption cake with your name
Lives that will never, ever, be the same.

■

11

Family Day and Adoption Day

As predicted, the legal adoption was a landmark. Finally, after three years, we arrived at our legal adoption day and celebrated in a large hired hall. It was Emily's choice to do it this way rather than spend a weekend at Disneyland Paris, or to celebrate as a family in some other way. Emily wanted to share this important event in style – she's a real party animal! In fact, the legal process being what it is, we actually celebrated a month before we went in front of the judge, which we hoped would merely be a formality. It was. The judge was delightful, and Emily so relaxed because of his paternal manner, that she started clowning and took his wig off and placed it on her own head! The judge commented: 'What a lovely, but clearly wilful girl she is; you've got a real handful there! She'll need watching!'

With the many photos we had taken during our three years and three months together, we created posters with captions to place all around the room. One of my sisters brought a cake iced with "Happy Adoption Day". Many friends and family helped and everyone gave Emily a gift.

I think she felt like a real princess that day. Some of the decorations hanging from the walls and ceiling were heart cushions, which were then given to the children to take home as mementos. Many tell us that they have theirs still.

Even now, Emily talks about this party with huge affection and I'm so glad that we chose to mark the occasion in this way and to show everyone how very important our daughter is to us and how proud we are of her.

Every year we celebrate the day we came together as "Family Day" by having a party at home with a few friends and relatives. As it takes place in the summer, we've usually been lucky enough to be in our garden. One year we took a friend's parachute out to the local park and listened to the shrieks of delight as each child in turn was thrown up in the air.

Emily's special gift on her fourth Family Day was a rabbit – she now has three but the one in the poem below is definitely the "celebrity" as he's so feisty!

HAPPY

4th

Family Day

My rabbit

by Emily

He stomps around all day
Because he never gets his way
He jumps up and down
Never round and round
He scamps from place to place
He has a cute face
And his name is
SCAMPERS!

Number bonds

1 + 1 and your brother was born
1 + 1 and you joined him
Only you were sick and needy
So you barely counted;

You didn't figure in anyone's mind.
Then 1 + another 1
And a sister arrived
Followed by another.

4 now, but your brush with death
Times 2 almost made it 3.

But still the 1 +1 didn't count the 4
And left them alone in their meagre room.
So strangers came to take you away
And the 4 of you were divided.

You don't want it this way
The other three still count for you
But you need an exclusive two
And a home where you will always be
NUMBER ONE.

12

Brother and sisters

The day after our adoption had become legal I met my daughter at the gates of her primary school. On this day there was no greeting, no kiss, no cuddle from my usually affectionate girl but what I can only describe as an "explosion" of the worst fury ever: 'If they wanted me to be specially looked after, don't they know that my brother did that for me and my sisters, and he can still do that? Those stupid people!'

On and on she yelled. Her arguments were clear, reasoned and extremely well-articulated – she hated, with a passion, the social workers she thought had taken her away from her beloved brother and sisters. I felt impotent in the face of her rage. I also felt that what she was saying made a lot of sense.

Her anger did eventually abate, although she is still given to rants from time to time. Yet the vital importance of her siblings, especially her brother, was something I understood even more acutely on that day; a day, it should be said, when everything was sealed and our daughter was secure in the knowledge of the legally binding commitment we had made to her. Thus she felt safe enough to give full vent to her anger for the very first time. Until that point, all her energies had gone into ensuring that we were hers and that we would not reject her and send her away.

I wrote *Number bonds* reflecting upon what our daughter had been through. In the early stages of the adoption I was unable to relate her personal history to close family and friends without becoming tearful about the enormous loss she continued to feel, particularly with regard to her separation from her siblings. Emily was learning about number bonds at primary school, and one evening the two just came together in my head in the poem. Emily still struggles a great deal to cope with the acute pain she feels as a consequence of living without her brother and two sisters.

Her yearning for her brother is stronger than anything. After a few months have gone by without contact, Emily's mood fluctuates and she often cries to see him. She misses him desperately and pines before our very eyes. Her frustration and anger at the situation naturally focuses on us, although she knows intellectually that we are not responsible. She is getting better at trusting that we do all we can. Emily is desperate to be with her brother, despite being happy and loved within our family, and we ensure she has regular contact, which now includes longer reciprocal visits. In some ways this appears to have helped Emily and in other ways it has increased her longing to be with her brother on a permanent basis. What is amazing, however, is that she says she would not live with him if she could because she would miss us!

—■—

Mother in mind

The wicker basket which she carried,
her warm smile beaming above,
pristine court shoes clicking below:
Busy, purposeful, loving.

The wicker basket which you carry,
your sleepy gaze frowning above,
scuffed black shoes kicking below:
Angry, reluctant, ignoring.

Back from work,
replenish the fridge,
back from school,
replenish my heart

with your warm soup,
your beaming afternoon smile.
Light from another life
filling my head with hope.

13

Mother's Day: Joy and wondering

My third Mother's Day was one of the best days of my life: I got three cards from my ten-year-old. She wrote "I love you" in big letters inside one of the two she made herself. She gave me a bunch of my favourite coloured tulips, made and tied a paper flower to my bed, and brought me breakfast.

This would be special enough from a birth child but to me it was a minor miracle: I never realised until our daughter joined our family just how much it means to hear a child call you "Mum" or "Mummy", or in my daughter's case, a very endearing "Mama".

I suppose I was lucky that my daughter called me "Mum", or variations of it, from the outset. Having said that, it felt somehow "borrowed" at that point, as though we were both role-playing a little. In a way we were. I have noticed how progressively "mum" has sounded more real, like my daughter now actually believes it.

'After a time, you forget that you are adopted,' wrote Emily in an English lesson at the start of secondary school.

After the legal adoption, Emily would pout like a toddler, and glower at any other child I might be talking to amongst a group of friends or family – 'My mama,' she would say. She would physically obstruct access to me by placing herself in between me and another child. It took another year of constant reassurances before this stopped.

Mother in mind was written because Emily was getting ready for cooking at school one day and I offered her my mum's wicker basket. Emily was delighted to use it to keep her cookery ingredients upright. That day they were making leek and potato soup in her Food Studies lesson. As she walked away it reminded me of how my mum used to carry the basket and how smartly she would be dressed for work. I thought about our three generations and how, even though my mum is no longer with us, in some ways I was connecting with her. The last line is both the light and the optimism from the life I shared with my mum and the light and hope given to me by my daughter – and, hopefully, from me to her.

The poem, *Baking for life,* celebrates my Emily's relationship with her second Granny by adoption! Whereas Granny Sue lives more than two hours away, Granny Doris is just a few doors down the road. My daughter often flies in from school and straight out again to go and visit her preferred haven and drink tea from china cups and saucers on little tables in front of the cosy gas fire, whilst listening to stories from this remarkable, now 86-year-old woman. Granny Doris is always busy knitting for various great-grandchildren and has shown infinite patience in teaching my daughter this skill. My daughter also loves baking cakes with her Granny or working in her very well-tended and abundant garden. She has been a wonderfully calming and nurturing influence in Emily's, indeed in all our lives, ever since.

'Why do you want to go down to Granny Doris so much?'

'I like it; it's quiet and Granny Doris's stories are interesting.'

There is something very reassuring for her about this wonderful woman who always has a project on the go in which Emily can easily involve herself and about which there is no time pressure.

The following poem with its somewhat corny rhymes was written to try and amuse Emily and with some suggestions from her! It does, however, accurately represent Emily's dynamic and sympathetic grandma.

■

Your granny

Doris is your adopted Granny at number 34
A Granny and a Great-Gran to more.
When I first wrote the letter
Wanting to make life better
I never knew that she sang in a choir
Nor sat for hours by the fire
Recycling Christmas cards for sailors.

That she gave talks three times a week
And blithely baked cakes for all to seek
at her local church Bring and Buy.
I never knew how well she tended her flowers
How perfectly she deals with life's showers
How intact her memory of our street
How enthusiastically she chats when we meet
And I am so glad that a wise good woman of 85,
Who has her own already, helps my one to thrive!

■

Baking for life

Green fingers guiding yours
as you cast
a stitch in time until the cake
has been made and you can
lick the bowl
of your own dreams.

My mum

by Emily

My mum is so beautiful
My mum is so magical
She is super mum
She takes me on outings
I love my mum and you know what?
She loves me and always will

■

Days when you make me feel invisible

You have
taken over
our lives,
got inside
our heads,
our hearts,
every minute
of every day.

This morning
you sulked;
went unwillingly
to school.
In the playground
for ten minutes
or more
while you
hung
your
head
right
down,
shutting me out.

Tried to
make you
smile
but
failed.
You said,
'I don't have to.'

A teacher smiled,
'I'll take her in.'

You did not
even
give me
a cursory
glance
and I
became invisible:
a strange woman
in a strange land.

I walked
away
leaving my life
my head
my heart
in torment.

■

14

Coping with changes

After over five years of living with my daughter, it has struck me that almost everything we do is geared towards equipping her to deal with change so that she can move forward and out of some of the "coping" patterns that have stuck since she was a baby and a toddler. This kind of nurturing is not easy when you're beginning it at age seven and it requires a lot of support, patience and resourcefulness. Broadly, the three poems in this chapter cover the most difficult changes: primary school, night-time and the transition from primary to secondary school. Within each of these there are a myriad of complex emotions at work for both our daughter and ourselves.

Primary school

Going to a different primary school with different faces in a different part of the country where the children have a different accent, setting out from a different home, with a different "mammy" walking you to school down a different road, past a different park makes a big DIFFERENCE to how you feel!

We chose our daughter's primary school partly on the positive recommendation of our social worker. The Learning Mentor played a key role in helping Emily to integrate into her new school. As well as getting a boost from the dance classes and the shows that she organised, our daughter developed a close and extremely positive relationship with the Learning Mentor, as did we, which became crucial when Emily was particularly anxious or upset.

In general, Emily struggled with feeling unhappy during much of her time at primary school. A lot of this unhappiness stemmed from desperately wanting to make friends, missing her siblings, and just generally adapting to her new home and family. The Learning Mentor kept a special eye on Emily at break and lunch times in the early days. Initially, Emily preferred to offer to help her teachers rather than go out and try to play with other children. She suffered quite a lot of name calling and although she would defend herself and give as good as she got, she would often break down in tears as soon as I met her, over some remarks that had been made – about being adopted, having a different accent, or something else. We would role-play imaginary situations to give her some positive ways of dealing with hurtful comments.

'Ms Lomas, can we have a word in my office, please? Emily, if you'd like to stay and help Mrs Simm tidy the reception area books while your mummy and me are talking?'

I don't know which of us felt more like a child at that moment.

These "words" with the Head happened fairly frequently. 'Emily seems to be having a lot of arguments with the boys. They don't like her telling them what to do as if she were another teacher in the room.'

I remembered Emily's complaints about the boys and the tears at the school gates on a number of occasions.

'Yes. She does find the boys in the class naughty. She's finding it hard to make friends with the girls, too, given that they formed friendships in Year 1 and she lacks these social skills.'

There were only six girls in the whole class! Emily was desperate for a friend. 'Actually,' continued the Head, 'I think we need to do more to help her use her need to be in charge ("PC-speak" for "bossiness", I thought!) and her emotional need to be among younger children. How would you feel about her going over to reception class for the first 20 minutes of every afternoon? She tends to play with these children at break-time anyway and she could help them.'

This proved to be a brilliant idea and Emily enjoyed the responsibility as well as deriving a lot of emotional comfort from being with the "little ones" who loved her, as she has a strong maternal and caring side. This, in turn, boosted her poor self-esteem and helped her towards peer friend-ships.

So much about coping at school and making friends was beyond my con-trol that it made me feel useless and incompetent. The times when I could do nothing to appease her deep sadness made me feel the enormity of what we had taken on: I was getting nowhere and going nowhere; I could be any woman to this little girl – not a mother but a stranger, unable to help.

Days when you make me feel invisible was written after the legal adoption, after the "honeymoon", after I was sure we had bonded, after the perfect "Gift" moment. The despair in the poem reflected one of my lowest times.

It took almost three years before Emily slept with her fists unclenched and

■

Night time

Night time

The most important time?

Time of cuddles and stories and cosiness.

Time to feel safer than ever.

Or a time of being alone; lonely; frightened?

A time of being in the dark.

A time of being left alone with thoughts...

you'd rather not have.

■

before she would sit up with a start from being asleep even if I trod lightly to go and check on her, particularly in the early days when I must admit to being like a mother with a new baby and worrying that she was still breathing.

I remember the first time I saw her fists unclenched and then the first time I saw her sleeping with her arms up beside her ears as carefree babies do. I took it as a sign that she felt truly safe at last and felt so relieved and happy.

Emily has a leopard and two bears who have voices (mine) and to whom she is mother but who take care of her at night. I tell stories with these furry animals when my daughter is preparing to go to sleep. These stories usually recount what has happened in my daughter's day, for example, they bring a friend home for tea, eat, do an activity, prepare themselves for bed and are then tucked in. This bedtime routine, like the milk, then more milk, and the stories and/or poems from her favourite collection have helped to reassure her.

Moving from primary to secondary school

Once again the struggle here was down to the discrepancy between Emily's emotional and chronological ages, so much so that we did have very serious discussions with the Primary Head as to whether Emily should repeat Year 6. In the end, the decision was made that it would not, overall, be in her best interest. Emily, herself, was keen on repeating as she felt "too little" still and this agonising decision took months to make. The worry was that we might not have got it right – Emily's attitude at times in her first year made us feel that we hadn't. *Crossing the divide* is intended to reflect just that.

Goodbyes

There's a song about how hard this word is! Certainly in Emily's case it has been.

Emily formed a friendship with the girl next door, which lasted until she started secondary school one year ahead of Emily. They did not attend the same primary school but saw each other intermittently at weekends. They would alternate playing in each other's houses and we two mothers would ensure safe transition to and fro. At first , when Emily was collected from next door she bit my stomach and screamed and cried. I thought the mother felt we must be such cruel parents; as if returning home to us was so awful! Once back with us she would be quite happy again, but the family next door didn't see that. They knew she was adopted and knew about her siblings but there was not the opportunity, nor the desire, to go into all the whys and wherefores. I suppose I just took the mother's reassurances that Emily could visit again as meaning she wasn't going to hold it against her and I was just desperate to take my distraught daughter back into our home where I knew I would be able to calm her down.

Crossing the divide

Started Secondary
but you're not ready.
Inside the gangly frame
your mind hurts
trying to keep steady.

How to play the grown-up game?

Inside the toddler rebels!
Yells!
Screams and whines at the sight of
HOMEWORK!

Rooms, bells, teachers, folders, books
lockers, rules, uniforms,
name tags, older girls' looks.

Where do I fit in?

Can I make friends?

Can I cope with all this?

'I want to go back to Primary!'

'I don't feel like a Secondary girl.'

I look at the frail pale creature saying the words,

feel her pain, and know she is right:

I can only try to help her cross

another

huge

divide.

■

Unconditional love

The sum of your parts
Laid out in squares on the table
Etched inside our hearts
The stuff of real life, not pretty fable.

There's your messy, couldn't care less part
Your dressy, sense of occasion, party part.
Your mad, sad, happy, snappy, bossy, busy parts
Your singing, dancing, painting, playing, swimming, cycling parts.
Your loving, giving, sharing, cuddly parts
Your tantrum-throwing, wilful, controlling parts.

Your sister to three part
Your living without them part.
Your Welsh part
And your London part.

Parts that you have lost
Parts that you have gained.
Parts that we are healing
Some only now revealing.

All parts that we are sewing
Piece by piece, into this quilt.

15

My daughter forever

Like every other adopted child, Emily has a life story book. To my knowledge, she has looked at it twice. At the moment she does not choose to keep it in her special bedside cabinet with her other albums, folders of birthday and Christmas cards, family and Adoption Day cards. It is clear that she is protective of us and her position within her "forever family" because she rarely mentions her birth parents. We know that she mentions them sometimes to others.

We have made it clear to Emily that we are happy to answer her questions and to talk with her about her birth parents. At the moment, on the rare occasions she refers to them, it is usually in reference to her height or other physical characteristics.

There are people, not adoptive parents themselves, who question the point of adoption if the child eventually goes to seek his or her birth parents. Emily's birth parents were not able to look after her and keep her safe. We chose to give total commitment to nurturing and loving Emily, providing the solid roots of parents who will always be there for her. We want her to make the best of her skills and talents as well as to keep her safe, well and happy on the way to what we hope will be a fulfilling life. We look forward to a long and enriching shared future. When she is old enough, it is possible that she may contact her birth parents in order to understand where she came from.

I'm happy and proud to be a part of my daughter's life and will be her mother forever. There is a genuine and loving bond between us and I will be privileged if she keeps a place for me in her heart and her home.

Unconditional love was, in part, inspired by a training day, "Adopted Children: Age and stage" run by Holly Van Gulden, to whom I am indebted for the positive differences she has helped me to make in the parenting of my daughter.

———■———

My mum

My mum is so beautiful

My mum is so magical

She is super mum

She tacks me onouting

I Love my mum and you

know what? She loves me
and alwas will.

To mama and Dady

I love you So much

Love you The whol of u:k
farm   ♥

My mum
gives me lots
of cuddels
and I love
her a lot
♥x

■

Bright light

The sun behind white winter clouds
The warm glint behind a loving eye

The gorgeous gurgle of a contented baby
The bliss of a daughter's trusting embrace

Bright light in a dark life.

■

my DaD and mum   my Diry

I Love my Mam and DaD
Im Adopted you know

16

Bright light

Bright light was the last poem I wrote when I began to collate the material for this book. It was written after a family visit to a friend living on the Sunderland coast. This very close friend has bipolar disorder and there have been times when her life has been very bleak. Her few weeks old beautiful baby girl was giving her such joy, hence the last line, 'Bright light in a dark life'.

This had an obvious meaning for me too. Our shared time made me reflect upon what both our lives had been like before we embarked upon motherhood and what our respective daughters mean to us.

We walked along the beach in the low-lying winter sunshine and her new baby gurgled contentedly as she talked to her. My 12-year-old hugged me.

I thought about how my friend's baby trusted her mother instinctively and how ecstatically happy I was that my daughter now felt safe and secure in my love and care.

Being adopted by
age 12

I have being adopted because
then you know you have
a family that loves you.
I have been with my mum
and dad for almost 6 years.
I like having a family that
is fun and now I am
having fun.